BOSTON AND THE FEAST OF ST. FRANCIS

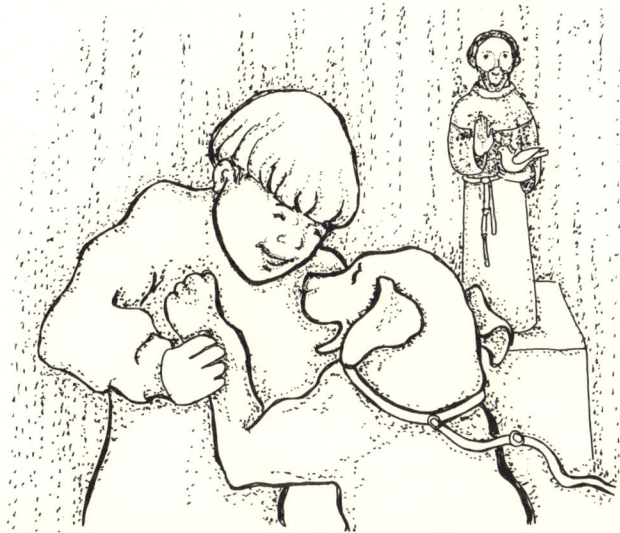

SUE STANTON

Illustrated by Jeanne Heiberg

PAULIST PRESS
New York, N.Y. ● Mahwah, N.J.

To the real Sam and his Boston
with love

ISBN: 0-8091-6616-X

Published by Paulist Press
997 Macarthur Boulevard
Mahwah, New Jersey 07430

Printed and bound in the
United States of America

Every year as long as Sam could remember, St. Cecilia's school celebrated the feast of St. Francis with a day set aside to bless the animals of the schoolchildren. It was a day in honor of the saint who was a friend to every living creature.

Before the day arrived, the children were invited to bring all their pets—fish, dogs, cats, gerbils—anything that was special to them.

Sam was excited this year. In the past, he had taken his stuffed squeaky dog, Minneapolis.

But now he was able to bring his very own tail-wagging, face-licking, people-thumping dog. Boston, his almost year old king-size rottweiler, would be blessed by Father Dismas. Sam could hardly wait!

One afternoon Sam lay beside Boston on the living room rug, looking straight into his glistening brown eyes.

"If I take you to be blessed for St. Francis' day, you will be good, won't you, Boston?"

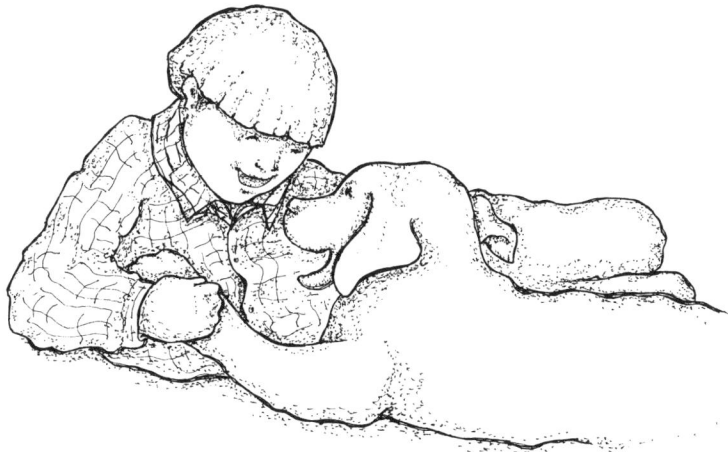

The large dog lifted his head and stared at Sam for a long moment. Snorting, he placed his head between Sam's hands, nuzzling his plaid shirt.

But Sam started to worry. Maybe his father was right. He said taking Boston to school for the blessing would be a disaster. Sam thought of how every night as soon as his father came in the front door, Boston would knock him down and lick his face.

"Get off me, you smelly beast!" Sam's father would shout as Sam pulled Boston from his father's chest.

What if Boston did the same thing to Father Dismas in front of the whole school?

That night Sam did not sleep a wink as Boston snored beside him. Watching Boston's large head lying on his own pink pillow, Sam remembered his mother fussing one morning.

"That animal should not be in your bed."

"If I had a brother, he'd have to sleep in bed with me, wouldn't he? So why not Boston?"

"Because you'd have a human being for a brother and not a dog. Boston is just a big dumb animal, and he belongs on the floor."

His mother didn't understand, Sam thought to himself. Boston is my brother. I had nobody until he came.

Sam decided that he had to make sure Boston did nothing wrong at the blessing.

Stopping in front of the school doors the next day, Sam gave Boston a pep talk. "You will remember to be good, now, Boston. Don't forget. It's really important!" Sam shook his finger in Boston's face as the dog shot out his long tongue and licked it.

Giving the dog a quick hug around the neck, Sam's fingers closed tightly on the leash and together they walked into school.

Boston followed Sam into the quiet school gym, but at the sight of the huge Boston the gym did not stay quiet for long!

All at once, the children's pets struck up a terrible racket. Birds in cages squawked and screeched, their bright feathers flying high in the air. A gray cat leaped from it's owner's arms and hopped from chair to chair. Three first-graders scrambled after a shivering calico kitten that scurried under a table. The boy sitting next to Sam held tightly onto his glass cage containing a white rat, it's long pink tail thumping and twitching against the sides of the glass.

Finally, Sister Clare gave a signal for quiet. Father Dismas came forward wearing a white robe tied at the waist with a rope. In front of him were two servers, helpers he would need to hold pets and leashes during the blessing.

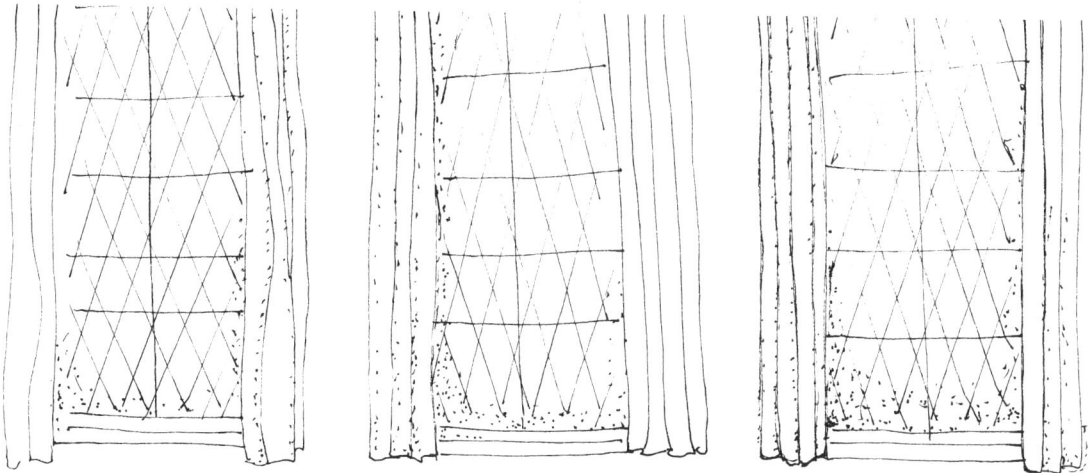

A white cloth placed on the top turned a teacher's desk into an altar and stood at the front of the gym. Two candlesticks glowed at each end, and Sam noticed their glow flickering in Boston's eyes.

Slowly the priest climbed the steps that led up to the altar and sat in an ancient wooden chair. All was quiet.

Standing, Father Dismas prayed, "St. Francis, we celebrate your friendship with all God's creatures and hope that you will grant them long life and happiness on this earth."

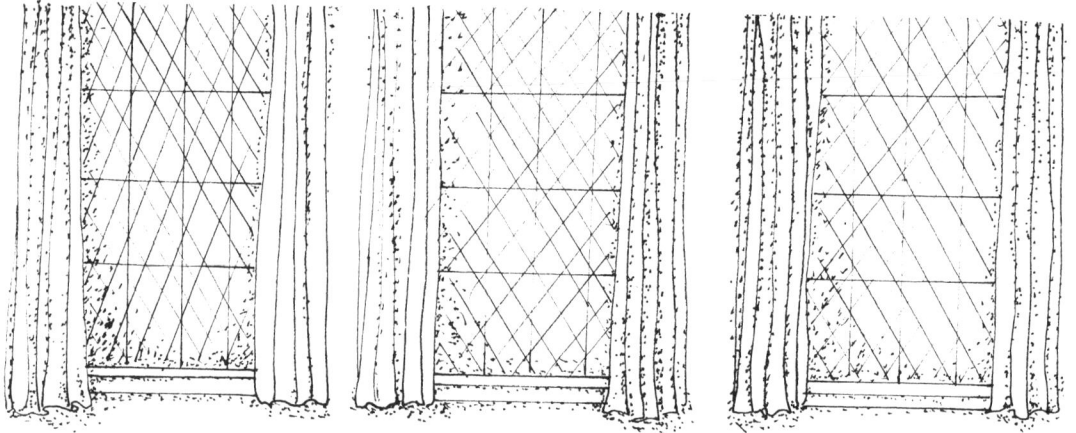

Just then, Pling! Plonk! The white rat shot out of its cage and landed on the chair in front of Sam. Two girls in front of him grabbed their feet as Sam dove for the rat just as it jumped onto another chair. But Sister Clare stepped over, and with one swoop, grabbed it by the tail and deposited the rat back in it's cage. It was only then that Sam remembered Boston. He had dropped the leash and Boston was gone!

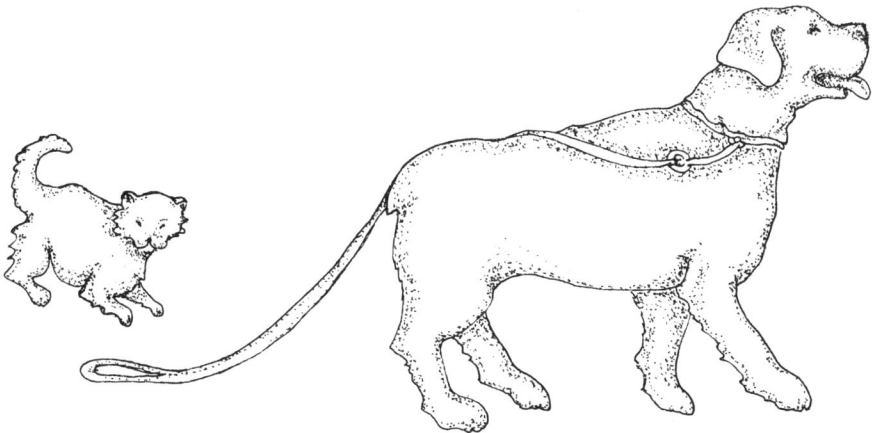

Sam looked toward the altar where Father Dismas stood with outstretched arms, a perfect target.

Boston, trotting down the aisle, stood at the bottom of the steps leading up to the altar and Father Dismas. Sam slid down in his seat. Oh no! He couldn't watch. Boston looked ready to spring!

All eyes left Father Dismas as one of the servers tried to shoo Boston back, waving his hands alongside the bottom of his chair. Boston climbed the steps and looking around once, twice at the crowd, headed straight for Father's ancient chair, plopping his back end onto it.

By now it was impossible not to notice Boston. He was part of the service!

Unaware, Father Dismas proceeded with the opening prayer. Boston cocked his head from side to side, watching the priest's hands go up and down, higher and lower, left and right. Boston licked his lips.

The first graders squirmed and giggled in their places, pointing their fingers. Father Dismas turned to where they pointed and started to laugh. Boston sat like a king on his throne, his tongue dangling off to the side. All the children, teachers and parents laughed, too. It was just like Boston. Father signalled for another chair to be placed beside the enormous dog.

Father Dismas sat looking into the large dark eyes of the dog facing him. After several minutes, Father stood and signalled again for silence.

"I want to tell you all," he began, "that this is a special moment for me. This dog has shown us exactly how St. Francis would have conducted the blessing. St. Francis would bless villagers as well as their cows, sheep, donkeys and pets. He would bless the birds of the forest and the wolves in the hills near his home in Assisi. When he stopped to rest, the animals would come to sit near him. He would speak with them and bless them. St. Francis felt we should celebrate all of God's creation, humans and animals alike. It is good for you to be sitting right where you are, fella. This is the way the blessing of St. Francis should be." Father Dismas patted Boston's head as the dog licked his arm.

"Will this fella's owner come forward, please?"

Sam proceeded slowly toward the steps, afraid to make any sudden movements for fear Boston would lose the hold he had on his good behavior.

Finally, Sam reached the steps and climbed up to face Father Dismas and Boston.

"What's your friend's name, Sam?" Father asked.

"Boston" Sam whispered.

Boston moved out of the chair and over to where Sam stood. Father Dismas, placed a hand on each head and spoke in a loud voice, "According to St. Francis, we are all one with God's creatures. We are as one brother and sister to each other. Each of us is pleasing to God just as he has created us. So may the blessing of St. Francis be upon you, Sam, and upon your brother, Boston. May you have long life and happiness together."

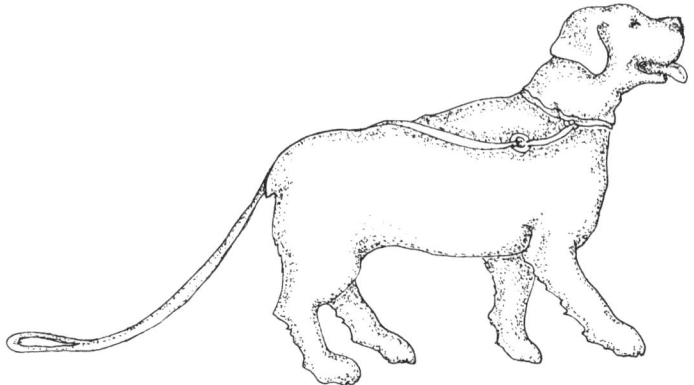

Sam's face beamed as Boston licked his cheek.
I knew it, Sam thought, I knew it all along.
Boston and I, brothers at last!